T0171717

YES, I CAN.

ACADEMIC GUIDEBOOK FOR COLLEGE SUCCESS.

DAVID S. KYERE

FOREWORD BY
DR. VINCENT NARTEY KYERE

*author*HOUSE®

AuthorHouse™
1663 Liberty Drive
Bloomington, IN 47403
www.authorhouse.com
Phone: 833-262-8899

Published by AuthorHouse 06/23/2023

ISBN: 979-8-8230-1084-9 (sc)
ISBN: 979-8-8230-1086-3 (e)

Print information available on the last page.

This book is printed on acid-free paper.

CONTENTS

Dedication vii

Foreword ix

Introduction xi

Chapter 1   Understanding Your Professors and Their Classes 1

Chapter 2   Combining College Work and a Job 11

Chapter 3   Preparing and Going According to your Personal
Planned Schedule 19

Chapter 4   Adopting Strategies to Study 31

Chapter 5   Preparing for and Excelling at Exams 41

Acknowledgements 49

Special Thanks 51

DEDICATION

To my wife, Mrs. Ama Kesewa Kyere, a paraprofessional at New York City's department of education, and to my intelligent son, Joshua Quaye Nkunim Kyere, a future clergyman and academician.

To my parents, Mr. Anthony Kwaku Kyere and Mrs. Agnes Abena Kyere, both retirees of the ministry of education in Ghana.

To all college students and alumni of Jehovah Rapha Prayer Ministry International in Bronx, New York.

To all college students and alumni in the world.

FOREWORD

by Dr. Vincent Nartey Kyere

David S. Kyere is my younger brother, and I respect him for his professional competence in handling issues of tutoring, educating, and guiding students in general, and college students in particular, to cope with the myriad challenges that confront them in their day-to-day routines. Over the years I have followed my brother's professional progress with keen interest, and I have come to the conclusion that he is on top of his game when it comes to providing the right information to help learners combine their studies with their jobs and get the best out of their endeavors.

His book *Yes, I Can: Academic Guidebook for College Success* is tailored toward satisfying the needs of college students who combine work with their studies. Such students have to know what professors require of them and be responsive to those demands. The students have to know how to use their time judiciously in order to make the most out of their busy schedules. Equally important is being equipped with the relevant skills of learning and preparing well to pass examinations.

It is my hope that readers will find useful information in the pages of this book that will help them reach their aspirations in this fast-changing world. Learning and working simultaneously have become part and parcel of human endeavors, and any effort to help students find an easy way out of the challenge is welcome news. This is where David S. Kyere's book will come in handy.

INTRODUCTION

Yes, I Can: Academic Guidebook for College Success is designed to help students understand what professors want. It will help them get good grades, acquire metacognitive skills (problem-solving abilities), develop good habits, and get good recommendations and strong networking.

Students have all it takes to be successful in college and beyond. This guidebook will teach students how to strategize, adopt study skills, and—above all—cooperate with their professors in order to gain the skills they need to succeed in all areas—not only for their schooling years, but also in their future lives.

This book includes many well-proven strategies to help students combine their academic, research, and working activities while attending college.

CHAPTER ONE

Understanding
Your Professors
and Their Classes

1. Introduction

- It's very important to understand your professors and the nature of their classes.
- You must be attentive in your classes and give special attention to professors' instructions.
- Remember that most professors want their students to get good grades, graduate from school, receive awards and scholarships, find good jobs, and realize their dreams.
- Professors are unique individuals, and it's up to you to really know the goals of each class and meet those expectations. That is the secret of becoming successful in courses you're taking and beyond.

2. Respect Your Professors

- Professors play very important roles in their students' lives and must be accorded the respect they deserve. Show professors respect in the same way you show respect to your parents and other caretakers.

- Get to know and work with your professors while respecting the boundaries they've put in place. Respecting boundaries is especially important in student-faculty relationships and will help your future work relations.

- If you show respect to your professors, some may share their phone numbers or personal email addresses with you. This can help you communicate with your professor even when you're off-campus—for example, if you need urgent help with an assignment or project. Don't abuse this type of gesture by reaching out unnecessarily; your professors aren't your friends.

- Don't be rude to your professors, thinking you are exercising your fundamental human rights. Always speak to them politely, and don't ever raise your voice with them. If you don't agree with a professor's views, be sure to articulate your opinion respectfully.

3. Relating to Professors

- Most professors are keenly interested in interacting with their students; after all, they've chosen a profession in which they lecture and teach. As such, professors are generally sociable by nature and will likely be able to relate to you well.

- Learning to relate to your college professors might end up being one of the most rewarding skills you can gain during your time in school.

- Since classes often take place in lecture halls with a large number of students, it's impossible for every lecture to resonate on a personal level with everyone. Don't let this make you feel intimidated in the presence of professors, as they are human and will understand your needs.

- Attend classes regularly, and don't be absent without a good reason. If you are sick or have an emergency that keeps you from making it to class, send the professor an email explaining your absence in advance.

- Send your professors news articles about important issues relating to subjects you've discussed in class.
- Attend office hours and meet with professors after class if you have any questions or problems.

4. Participate in Class and Coursework

- Class participation consists of more than just sitting down and taking notes while your professor lectures.
- College requires you to engage with texts and other materials you cover and actively participate in class discussions.
- Prepare for each class by reading in advance, noting down points and questions, and being ready to participate. You should contribute meaningfully to every in-class discussion.
- If your professor assigns a group project, be actively involved. Sometimes your grade depends on these group projects. Your professor might be watching you from afar—you never know.
- Class participation benefits you and other students, as well as your professors. It also serves as feedback for professors on how students are feeling about topics being taught and discussed.
- Many professors give points or marks for class participation, as they know teaching shouldn't be a one-way process. Your contributions may also help others learn something new.

Class participation is required for both college and graduate degrees. Most professors base 10 to 20 percent of your grade on class participation—an amount significant enough to easily affect your final results. Always ask your professor whether your class participation is good enough.

5. Submit Your Assignments on Time

- Depending on your professors, you may receive online or paper assignments. These assignments aren't meant to punish you, but to allow you to demonstrate what you have learned to your professor.
- Some professors give full credit for assignments submitted on time. Avoid procrastinating so you don't end up feeling pressured right before the deadline.
- Usually deadlines for assignments help professors give you feedback and also restructure lessons before the next class.
- Be very cautious when submitting online assignments, as professors might not give you a chance to redo work. Don't click *submit* before you are sure you're done.
- Check the stated time for each assignment, and be sure to work within those parameters to avoid being shut out of the system completely. Late assignments might attract penalties or deductions and affect your grade at the end of the course.
- Professors want you to submit assignments on time because they are shaping you for the future. The same skills will likely be needed in whatever companies and institutions you work for.
- Professors give deadlines and may warn you that your work won't be considered if submitted late. They do this because if you complete assignments on time and avoid procrastination, there is a higher chance you'll grasp the concept.
- When you don't study and complete assignments on time, you tend to forget what was taught in class. When you submit assignments on time, it helps both you and your professor stick to the syllabus.
- Late assignments always affect professors' grading times and draw the class back, as questions will have to be answered about mistakes from previous or late assignment.

6. Talk to Your Professors about Improving Your Grades

Students often work and take classes at the same time. The burden of having a job and loads of assignments to complete isn't easy. Emergencies may also cause distractions in planned schedules. If you experience either of these scenarios, you might miss some classes or fail a test. Explain your situation to your professors, and find out what you can do to improve your grades.

One time I was admitted to the hospital for five days and missed a whole week of classes, including an important quiz in one. I spoke to the professor and showed him my medical records, and he simply asked that I watch a video and write an essay on it to make up for the quiz.

- Remember you can get such favors from your professors when you have tangible reasons, good behavior, and are a good class participant.
- Don't refuse to participate fully in a group project. Engage in proper consultation with the professor so you can gain good grades. Address any problems the group encounters in every stage of the project, and do not wait until the end of the semester.
- If you realize your grades are low, speak to your professor immediately. Do not wait for the end of the semester to explain yourself, as that will be too late. Even if you have a good reason, it will be difficult for your professor to accept that in the later part of the semester.

- Your grades for fall 2009

Course	Midterm Grade	Final Grade
ESE 11	D+	B-
ESE 12	B	A- (Good luck to you. Hope you take part in the Colorado program.)
ESE 13	D+	B

Your academic standing is good.

1. **Good academic standing**
2. **Early warning standing**
3. **Probation one (you are allowed to register seven credits per term)**
4. **Probation two (you are allowed to register seven credits per term)**
5. **Probation readmit (you are allowed to register seven credits per term)**
6. **Suspension (you are not allowed to register, but you can appeal)**
7. **Dismissal (you are not allowed to register for good)**

This is the first class I took at the Bronx Community College. ESE 11 and 13 were by Professor Farnosh Saeedi and ESE 12 by Professor Philip Neal. I did not do well on the midterm at all; it was almost a failing grade. I went to their offices and spoke with them about what I could do to improve my grade, and they took me through the course syllabus and explained what their expectations were and how to do their assignments, laboratory work, and exams. Their advice finally helped me do better, and I got the chance to be part of a weather-station program in Colorado. Look at Professor Neal's comment on ESE 12.

7. Be Punctual at All Times

- Each professor has an attendance policy. If you don't arrive on time for your classes, points might be taken off. Spend some time reading the policies for each class, and be punctual.
- College courses are packed with information, so coming late or leaving early can cost you. A whole chapter might be taught in one day when you don't show up. Every minute counts in college. Don't joke around with your life, and be punctual.
- If you are using public transportation, leave at least an hour early to avoid delays. It's better to be in class early than to have to rush and put yourself in a hectic situation—and still be late for class. You might become nervous, confused, stressed, and lost in the class if you are late.
- Students can now check schedules of public transportation online. For example, students at New York City can go online.

8. Pay Attention

The use of cell phones is the number one reason students have trouble paying attention in class. Professors can easily identify those who are not paying attention, despite distracted students thinking they have hidden their phone use. Students who use phones to check social media or play games tend to miss important points professors or classmates make and are not likely to do well in class.

Be focused while you're in class, and don't allow others to distract you when your professor is teaching. Avoid talking to classmates when class is going on so you don't miss any meaningful discussion. Checking and replying to text messages or using cell phones can change your As to Cs. In other words, the use of phones in class is directly proportional to bad grades.

- Avoid passing notes on to your friends, and don't reply if you receive any from classmates while class is in session.
- Write down some points in your notebook if you think you will forget.
- Avoid discussion with classmates while lectures are going on.
- Write down the things you need to do for each class in your assignment book, and make sure you update it after the lessons.
- If the lecture is boring and you feel like sleeping, get permission to do some body exercises or stretching to keep your mind active. It's not illegal.
- Students must concentrate and avoid reading other materials during lessons. Outside books should not be read while classes are going on.
- Phones should be turned off or put on silent during lessons to avoid distractions.
- Make sure you ask the professor to explain areas you don't understand before the next lesson or topic.

9. Ask Questions if You Don't Understand

- Feel free to interrupt your professor—especially if you don't understand something he or she said.
- Don't be intimidated by your professors or classmates, and remember that there's no such thing as a stupid question.
- If you're unclear about something the professor says during class or about the lecture, ask for clarification.
- Asking questions helps you remove doubt and gives the professor a chance to give further details.
- It is also a way of staying connected to your professor and indicating you are following the class with keen interest and attention.
- Don't assume you know everything and sit quietly. Let your voice be heard.

10. Attend Your Professors' Office Hours

Too many college students don't visit their professors' offices regularly or at all. Office hours give students the chance to talk to their professors on a more personal level and articulate certain concerns.

- It is a time to get to know professors better and find out more about class or course requirements. Questions that couldn't be answered in class can be followed up on during these hours.
- Registration of classes and scholarship or internship opportunities can be discussed with your professors at these times.
- Ask your professors if you need appointments to see them during office hours or if you can just walk in anytime.
- Be ready and plan your questions ahead so you don't block other students' chances to speak with professors during office hours.

11. Send Your Professors an Email after Registering for Their Classes

It's always important to send your professors an email ahead of your first class. You familiarize yourself with each professor as you introduce yourself to him or her.

When I was in city college, I always sent my professors an email once I'd registered for their class. I mentioned my name when we were introducing ourselves on the first day of class, and one professor exclaimed, "Oh, David, how are you?" We had already established a personal connection.

Sometimes I'd even go and visit professors in the office to ask them about assignments and expectations for the course. Try it, and you will see the results.

CHAPTER TWO

Combining College Work and a Job

1. Introduction

- In America and other developed countries, many students work while in college to pay tuition, hostel rent, and other utility bills.
- Other nations have subsidized college education, allowing students to study full time and lessening the demands on their time.
- Working and attending school at the same time comes with great advantages or opportunities; however, there are some challenges. There are so many cases in which the work being done isn't related to a student's major, and that can be more challenging.
- There are other instances where work may be related to a student's area of study, which allows them to get a degree while gaining some work experience.
- The good news is the company could end up hiring their student workers permanently or even promoting them.
- A challenge for the student can be combining the two and coming up with strategies to succeed in both.

2. The Demands of the Job

- It's difficult to balance work and college life. It is up to you to find meaningful ways to balance the two. You must know which is your priority.
- In my opinion, higher education is more likely to get you a better job in the long run, and knowing that's your priority will help you devote more time to school work, rather than your job.
- I advise students whose jobs are very demanding to move to another department or work part-time.
- Demands from jobs can make students tired and unable to concentrate during classes.

3. Take Note of the Type of Work and School Activities You Schedule

- Consider the number of credit hours you intend to take before attempting to apply for certain kinds of jobs.
- Consider your major and the content of your classes before making any decisions for a certain job.
- Most classes require laboratory work, essays, and projects and are very intensive, so the volume of work may be too much to combine with certain jobs.

4. Organize Yourself Well

- Keep your textbooks, handouts, and any other materials organized in a particular location. This will help you find them easily when you need them.
- Take note of due dates from your professor and start your assignments at the first opportunity.
- Keep all your materials filed and link them to your textbooks and notebooks.
- Use a to-do list to help plan and organize yourself well. You should know what you're supposed to do each hour of the day.

5. Use Your Time Wisely

- Now that you have college work and a job, you'll want to use your time wisely and not waste it. You have a lot to do, so use what's available the best way you can.
- Avoid procrastination and use the smallest amount of time possible on each task. For example, while you are on the bus or train commuting to school or work, you can start working on an assignment.

I used to commute an hour and forty-five minutes from my house to school and often worked on assignments or manuscripts for my books. While I was in college and working at the same time, I mostly did my assignments during my hour lunch breaks. It was a very effective way of using my time.

Students can waste a lot of time looking for the right notebooks and handouts before going to class. Keeping a folder and a notebook preferably the same color. This will will help you be more organized and easy to find your notebooks and handouts without going through difficulty

6. Plan and Keep a Schedule of Your Activities

- You must have a good schedule that helps you combine all your activities.
- All your work and school activities should be put down on paper or on your phone. Be diligent, and go according to your planned schedule.

To make planning your schedule workable, take note of the following:

- If you work at night, you should not register for early morning classes. Choose classes in the afternoon instead. Registration for classes early will help in this regard.

- Going to school right after work will not be helpful. You'll be tired and unable to focus or concentrate and may not stick to your schedule.
- Schedule your time such that there will be some time between school and the job.

Chapter 3 explains more about planning your schedule.

7. Using a Remembrance Book

- Using what I call a *remembrance book* can help you summarize your notes from studies and lectures, making it very simple and easy to study and remember.
- The content of the remembrance book is the framework of the whole subject matter. To make it simpler, go through your notes and textbooks and write down the main points.
- Summarize what your professor and classmates discussed in class into simple points. Once you see the summary of your notes in your remembrance book, the whole idea of the topic will come to mind.
- In reality, the book serves as the skeleton, or framework, for the entire subject matter. Although you did not study the whole chapter of your notes, the summary in your remembrance book keeps you from forgetting the whole concept.

Here's an example of an exam statement: write an essay explaining in detail the causes and effects of greenhouse gases.

- In order to answer, write the points on your question paper like the one in your remembrance book, and that will guide you to write your essay.
- Note that, once you remember these points, you will be able to explain answers in detail on an exam. When you remember

these summary points, you get something to say or write about the subject.

- You need the points, and the rest will be easy. *Write these notes in a booklet.* Start your own now. It is very easy to learn this way.

8. Use Remembrance Drawings

- Remembrance drawings are similar to the remembrance book. You make illustrations of certain features of your subject.
- These are very complicated features or processes in your course, or steps you need to know. Perhaps they are difficult to remember, so you draw or illustrate them on paper and put it up in your room so you can view it every day.
- Examples include: some major reactions in chemistry, the drawing of the eye in biology, Maslow's hierarchy of needs, or demand-and-supply curves in economics.
- A nursing student might draw the human eye and label all the parts and functions and place it on his or her door. The more they look at it, the more it enters their brain, giving a greater chance of remembering it at any time.
- You can always keep a copy of the remembrance drawings in your handbag, cell phone, bookbag, or pocket and view it when you have the chance.

9. Benefits of Remembrance Books and Drawings

- They make learning easier.
- They keep you from forgetting whole subject areas.
- They improve your memory because you can review them anytime.
- They are effective and convenient ways of studying anywhere.
- They can help you study even when you don't feel like it.

10. Contact Your Professors for Advice

- It is always good to seek counsel from your professors. A professor will help you understand the class you are about to take—whether it's demanding or writing intensive, if you can combine it with your current job, or if you'll get to speak to your professor for solutions and answers.
- How many classes can you take in total? Is there research work, internships, or project work connected to the class?
- You need to ask your professor all these questions before you make an attempt to register for classes.

11. Set Clear Goals for Yourself

Working full-time and going to school at the same time isn't easy at all. Students should set very clear expectations of how they'll spend their time. If you want to get good grades as a full-time worker, be diligent about your responsibilities by setting clear goals for your study and life.

- Example 1: I should finish my biology assignment by ten p.m. on Friday.
- Example 2: I should finish my prerequisite in two semesters.

12. Find Ways to Reduce Stress

- Remember you will be stressed if you want to be a student and a worker at the same time.
- Take advantage of holidays and days off to relax your brain and body. A good walk in the garden or a nearby park will be very beneficial.
- Hang out with family and friends on off days to reduce stress, or go to a park, concert, recreational center, or other fun places.

13. Remember to Exercise

- There are so many exercises you can do. You can ride a bicycle, run, or go to the gymnasium. Students need to maintain a healthy lifestyle at all times.
- Exercising reduces stress and laziness and makes you feel active and energetic. It can also make you flexible and even prevents diseases in certain cases.

14. Concentrate on the Most Important Thing

- Education is very important. You are going to school to make your life better, so most of your attention should be focused on it and not your job.
- After all, your employer could lay you off at any time. In no circumstance should you give your professors excuses for not doing your assignments because of your job.
- Even sports should not take precedence over you performing well academically. Prioritize your life, and do the most important things first.

15. Speak to Your Manager or Supervisor

- Speak to your supervisor at work about your school and the classes you are taking that semester. Inform him or her about the additional responsibilities of school while you are working there.
- Speak to your supervisor when midterm and final exams are around the corner.
- Managers must work out scheduling for you so you can adequately prepare for exams.
- Your supervisor might work something out and reduce the workloads or send you to another department that is less demanding.

CHAPTER THREE

Preparing and Going According to your Personal Planned Schedule

1. Aims and Objectives of Your Personal Planned Schedule

- Every planned schedule should have aims and objectives. In the first place, why do you need a planned schedule?
- Your planned schedule should serve a specific purpose for what you want to accomplish.
- The following are five samples of different planned schedules with specific objectives.

  - Example of specific objective of your planned schedule
  - Example and timetable sample 1
  - I want to pass my New York State Earth Science Test as part of my requirement for teacher certification K7–12 (summer timetable). —*David Garcia*
  - Example of a planned schedule sample 2
  - I want to pass and finish on time in my second year of school at Bronx Community College (fall semester timetable). —*Welbeck Sowah*

2. Important Notes before You Planning Your Personal Schedule

- There are important notes you should take into consideration when preparing your personal planned schedule.
- The objective of the personal planned schedule should be clearly stated, or you should at least have it in mind. Know why you're planning that schedule, and do it with determination.
- The objective of this timetable is to help you use your time wisely and achieve academic success.
- Another objective of making this planned schedule is to adopt strategies on how to combine school and work. Consider ways to become successful in school while you work to make some money to support yourself.
- Personal planned schedules should be time bound (spring semester or a three-month schedule).
- Time should be indicated for item or subject. For example: Psychology 101, 6–8 p.m. Time indication will make you more disciplined in moving from one subject or activity to the other.
- Include courses you were taught in class on your planned schedule. For example: every Friday you have Math 06 in the morning. Math 06 should be included in your schedule every Friday.
- Students should not pay special attention to some courses and leave the others. A failing course can affect your GPA.
- You should consider whether you are a slow or fast learner. Slow learners need more time to understand what is taught in class or what is being learned. In that case, you will need a lot of time for each subject. You can become a slow learner when you are not interested in a particular subject area.
- You should also consider whether you are a nocturnal or diurnal being—meaning whether you study best in the night or during the day time.

- If you are a night person, you should schedule most of your subjects later, and likewise, if you're a day person, plan for earlier classes.

- However, do not put reading subjects deep into the night. Most night periods are very cool and free from all distractions, so the chances that you will sleep and not study is very high. To avoid this, put mathematics or other subjects that will make you more active into the night schedule.

- You should include group discussion time in your personal planned schedule. You may also have to consider the time that will suit your other study mates as well.

3. How to Make Your Personal Planned Schedule

You can prepare your planned schedule by the following steps. The details of preparing a personal planned schedule have been outlined in my previous book *Yes, I Can: Guidelines for Studies for High School Students.*

First you need the materials.

- Materials will differ depending on the individual students. Some prefer to use a laptop, iPad, phone, or any device with a schedule planner. Others use Microsoft word or Excel or just a pen or pencil and A4 paper.

Special rules to guide you:

- Read the very important points to note before planning your personal schedule before this topic.

How to begin your timetable

- Get an 8½ x 11 size sheet or A4 paper, ruler, pencil, and your semester class schedule or work schedule.

- Get your laptop, iPad, cell phone or any device with a schedule planner.
- Read the important points to consider before you proceed to make the planned schedule.
- Draw seven even lines in rows using the landscape format of the paper. This applies to those using pen and paper.
- The first topmost space should be designated for date and time.
- The other lines represent the seven days of the week.
- You then have seven spaces left, so list the days of the week Monday to Sunday.
- Indicate time, subjects, and other activities clearly on your timetable.

4. Why Is It Important to Prepare Your Own Planned Schedule?

a. Helps You Use Your Time Wisely

- A lot of time is wasted every day because students do not plan and organize their school and life activities.
- They keep saying they are busy and only accomplish less work.
- Since time is a resource, it should be managed. The planned schedule will help you achieve this.
- The schedule helps you make the best use of the limited time you have.
- The planned schedule helps students to desist from unnecessary activities that waste students' time.

b. Motivates and Prompts You to Study

- You may not know how to transition from one activity to another. Having a planned schedule helps prompt you to study.

- Sometimes you feel lazy and don't know what to do. So many things pop up in your mind, but the planned schedule motivates you to study.
- Sometimes you don't feel like doing anything and just don't know why you should study. Once you see that you have planned your schedule, you will be energized to study.
- Social media can be an obstacle your studying. A planned schedule will help motivate you to study despite this.

c. **Directs Your Study**

- The planned schedule helps direct your study. Sometimes you feel like learning but don't know what to study or where to start from.
- The subject and time are written on the planned schedule. When you see the planned schedule it helps you know exactly what you should study.

d. **Helps You Combine Work and Sstudy Effectively**

- The planned schedule includes school and work activities. Transition from work to school can be challenging.
- The planned schedule helps you transition easily. You may become tired after work and spend a lot of time commuting.
- You get home and don't even know what to do. Look at your planned schedule, and it will help you do your next activity.

e. **Helps Plan Your Life**

- Having your personal planned schedule helps you to plan for life. Students who don't have a schedule wake up and don't know what to do.

- For instance, they might have evening or afternoon classes. The time before class may be wasted wasted because they don't have any planned activity to follow throughout the day.
- Having all of your activities written down will help direct your day. When you wake up and don't know what to do, go to your schedule and your day will be productive and well-planned.

f. It Helps You to Decide on What to Do Next

- The semester can become so stressful that you get caught up with what to do next. Having a personal planned schedule helps you make a decision without delay and wasted time.
- Sometimes you have three different assignments and don't know which one to start first. The schedule will help you decide in these times.

5. How to Stick to Your Planned Schedule.

a. Plan Daily

- Always review and go through your planned schedule every day to know your upcoming subjects and schedule so it becomes part of you.
- This will help you prepare ahead for any activities on your planned schedule.
- Look at the schedule, and view what subjects you have for the day.
- What are the topics you can study? Write those topics down.
- Do you have any quizzes that day or the next day you need to prepare for? List the topics you have to learn.
- How many hours of rest do you need for the day?
- How many hours of work do you have?
- How many hours will it take you to go home from work or school?

- Write all details of work and school on the to-do list.
- Remember: if you fail to plan, you plan to fail.

b. **Do Proper Evaluations of Your Studies and Activities**

- Evaluation simply means checking on whether you were able to do what you planned to.
- Why couldn't you do it, or why were you able to?
- If you couldn't do it or accomplish what you planned, what happened?
- Look out for what exactly went wrong. Some possible problems might be: laziness, lack of concentration, distractions by friends, excessive use of the internet, playing games, watching too much television, or lack of discipline.
- Try to deal with these issues so they don't prevent you from achieving what you plan to do the next day or the period of your planned schedule.
- If you were able to do as you planned, find ways of improving it so you achieve a greater performance the next day.

c. **Be Time Conscious**

- More details of this part will be shown under the effective way of using time.
- It simply means realizing you have something to do and responding quickly.

d. **Discipline Yourself**

- Students have many things they enjoy and have fun doing.
- It becomes difficult to change from one thing to another— especially at the time the activity becomes more interesting.

- Imagine yourself playing a videogame or swimming in a nice pool on a hot summer day. It's time for you to get up and go study or do your assignment, but of course that won't be easy.
- This is where discipline comes in—where you have to leave one thing to do the other, despite the fun or excitement.
- Discipline will deprive you of some pleasures but will make you achieve a desired goal and bring good results in the near future.

6. Things that Prevent You from Sticking to Your Planned Schedule

a. Work

Many students work while going to school. Sometimes they have to do overtime, and that might affect their planned studies.

b. Social Media

- It's difficult for most students to leave the computer and attend to their homework.
- Some programs like Facebook, Twitter, and Instagram keep students excited, and they spend a lot of hours there chatting, posting pictures, sending out videos, and viewing other people's profiles.
- Discipline is required to close these programs when it is time for studying.
- People are bored and emotionally weak. They always need someone to talk to or chat with. The use of social media helps, but excessive use of it is dangerous.

c. Technology

- Discipline yourself by watching television.

- Don't sit by your televisions while doing assignments. This makes your concentration low, and it takes you more time to finish.
- Make sure you watch television during your breaks, only as indicated in your planned schedule.
- In America most phone calls are unlimited. This means that the average student spends a lot of hours in the night on their cell phones. They tend to forget it is time for studies or homework.
- Students need discipline in these areas so they can concentrate on their academic work.
- Be bold enough and tell whoever is on the phone that it is time for you to study or do your assignment.
- In other cases you can switch off your cell phone when your planned schedule indicates a period of study to prevent any disturbances.

d. Personal and Family Issues

- Students who live with their families are sometimes overburdened with taking care of their siblings or other family members.
- Financial challenges of families—especially if parents are not working—can also be huge obstacles. Students may have to work extra to earn more, which will also affect their academics.
- Some family members may be sick, and students need to take some time off from work to care for them.
- Some are also going through difficult challenges, like immigration problems and legal battles, which might require students' attention.
- Personal or mental problems can lead to emotional problems, which causes obstacles to successful study.
- Each family has issues such as sickness, divorce, financial difficulties, mental illness, or even drug abuse that can be detrimental to students' academics.

- I advise students to find solution to these challenges or use the strategies discussed in this chapter to overcome or minimize both personal and family related issues.

e. **Procrastination**

- Procrastination is postponing an activity or what needs to be done now to the future or a later date.
- Students who often procrastinate forget what they need to do and miss deadlines. Students fail to do assignments and fail to meet professors' expectations.
- Procrastination looks very simple and easy to do, but students must know the effects in order to not do it just for fun.

People may procrastinate because:

- they have more time,
- laziness and reluctance,
- having loads of assignments,
- improper supervision,
- the teacher or person in charge is flexible,
- there's been an extended deadline, or
- there is no benefit for doing the task.

Consequences of procrastination may include:

- failing a class,
- difficulty catching up with classroom work and personal study,
- wasted time, and
- affecting your future career.

Avoid procrastination by:

- remembering that time is a resource that can be wasted,
- doing assignments bit by bit,

- doing some exercises to remove laziness,
- doing your work at the first opportunity,
- being aware of extended deadlines.

Do it now. Don't wait for it to impact your future.

Several environmental factors can also affect your academics, including lack of proper accommodations, transportation delays, bad weather, unfriendly campuses, and even lack of facilities.

Unexpected circumstances could occur, including:

- accidents or sicknesses,
- death of a relative,
- failure in initial or mid-semester exams, or
- other emergencies.

7. Examples of Personal Planned Schedules

Example 1

David Garcia has completed his bachelor's degree in Earth science. David wants to become a science teacher in the New York public school system. This schedule is to help him prepare for the New York State Earth Science Test as part of his requirement for teacher certification K7-12. (Summer timetable)

	9-10am	10-11am	11-12pm	12-1pm	1-2pm	2-3pm	3-4pm	4-5pm	5-6pm	6-7pm	7-8pm	8-9pm	9-10pm	10-11pm	11-12am
Sunday	Church	Church	Church	Church	Radio show	Visit hospital	Visit hospital	Visit hospital	Church	Church	Church	Church	Church	**READING**	
Monday	Work	Work	Work	Work	Work	Work	Work	Study	Study	Study	Study	Study	Study	READING	
Tuesday	Work	Work	Work	Work	Work	Work	Work	Study	Study	Study	Study	Study	Study	READING	
Wednesday	Work	Work	Work	Work	Work	Work	Work	Visit prisons						READING	
Thursday	Work	Work	Work	Work	Work	Work	Work	Study	Study	Study	Study	Study	Study	READING	READING
Friday	Work	Work	Work	Work	Work	Work	Work	Study	Study	Church	Church	Church	Church	Church	Church
Saturday	Relax	Relax	Relax	Relax	Relax	Study	Study	Study	Study	Study	Study	Study	Study	Study	Study

David S. Kyere

Example 2

Welbeck Sowah wants to pass and finish his associate's degree on time in a two-year college at Bronx Community College (fall semester timetable). Welbeck is a Kaplan Scholar and is preparing to enter medical school.

	9-10am	10-11am	11-12pm	12-1pm	1-2pm	2-3pm	3-4pm	4-5pm	5-6pm	6-7pm	7-8pm	8-9pm	9-10pm	10-11pm	11-12pm
Sunday	Housekeeping									Church					
Monday	Class				Revision and Studies			Class			Homework		Studies		
Tuesday		Class				Class				Tutoring			Mentor Office Hours Visit		
Wednesday	Class		Professor Office Hours Visit					Class					Assignment & Studies		
Thursday		Class	Club Meeting		Class					College Prep English Assignment			Leisure Hours		
Friday	Kaplan Leadership Program Workshop												Biological Research		
Saturday	Household Errands				Class Assignment					Workout Routine			Reading & Studies		

CHAPTER FOUR

Adopting Strategies to Study

1. Introduction

Adopting strategies to learn is a very important part of college students' lives.

2. Various Ways to Study

There's a need to adopt strategies to make your studies effective. There are so many strategies, but it will also depend on individual students and workers. This chapter will discuss many of these strategies to help the majority of students succeed.

a. Take Notes on Very Important Things the Teacher Brings Up

- Whenever a professor is lecturing, take notes on the most important things from the lesson.

- Sometimes the teacher stresses that students should take this part seriously. Write these notes down, and study them more to understand fully.
- When you write while the professor is teaching—even when you forget about some things—by referring to your notes you will remember.
- Remembering this important portion of your notes will help you in your study.

b. Use of Remembrance Books and Drawings

- The use of remembrance books in previous chapters, as well as in my previous book *Yes, I Can: Guidelines for Studies for High School Students.*
- Since the college is more engaged in other things, inclusion of this piece on remembrance books will help college students.

Note: Refer to chapter 2 for more information on remembrance books and drawings.

c. Group Discussion

- Group discussion is a very important strategy for learning.
- It assumes that each student has different levels of understanding the lessons taught by the teacher.
- Group discussion gives students an opportunity to share their ideas and put their thoughts together about a subject.
- There is brainstorming, concern building, and drawing of conclusions for everyone to understand.
- Strengths and weaknesses are raised, and each student is helped by bearing each other's burdens.

Group discussions are important, but let us go through some of the things you should take note of in group discussions.

i. Choosing People for Group Discussions

- The types of people chosen for group discussions is very important.
- You want people who are academically oriented, whose actions and moves show they're serious.
- The students must be in your class or doing similar courses, although your majors may be different.
- If you get a student with the same major that will be excellent since all subjects can be discussed.
- You must always get a leader to guide the group during the discussion session to maintain order and discipline.
- People of different races should be included without any discrimination whatsoever. Students should have people from different parts of the world to present in their groups.
- International students should be included if possible. Most international students may be doing similar courses that they have done in their home countries already, and they can bring their previous experiences into the group.

ii. Time for Discussion

- Students must consider which whether days or nights are more suitable for discussions.
- The time of the meeting must be specific and concise. For example: 6 p.m.–9 p.m.
- Begin the discussion promptly, and leave out unnecessary discussion that wastes time.
- The group discussion must relate to your classes, and the time should not conflict with lecture times.
- Use time wisely to benefit all.
- A summary should be done afterward.
- Avoid being late to prevent the discussion having to start again when someone shows up.

iii. Preparation for the Discussion

- Topics of discussion must be given to individual group members by the leader for them to study before the meeting. This makes the discussion very fruitful and productive, since students are prepared.
- Subtopics should be assigned to make further research and advanced studies. Each person can contribute what they learned to the discussion.

iv. Discussion Subjects

- Give out discussion subjects before meeting with group members.
- It's very important that each member has a fair idea of what will be discussed. Students can read ahead and prepare for the discussion. In this way each student makes a meaningful contribution, and everyone learns from each other.
- Some subjects can be decided on when you have a final exam/midterm exam or in relation to a project you are doing.
- More attention should be given to subjects in which the content is difficult to understand.
- Details and subtopics can also be given so that members can review.

v. Discussion Venue

- Since different students are meeting at the same time from different places, the venue should be centered for the benefit of all.
- If everyone resides at the school's campus, it is very easy to meet. However, I strongly recommend that nonresidents meet on school premises—especially when all have a class. This can be done in the library.

- The venue should be somewhere that allows each student to travel a short distance to get there.
- The venue should also be a discussion area. For instance, these are places of study where you can't afford to disturb other students who are quietly studying. Students can sit under a tree or go to areas designated for group study.
- The venue should be free from all distractions. Don't have group discussions near a football field, or you will always be distracted.
- In case of a change of venue, the leader should arrange for another venue or postpone the discussion after consulting all the other members.

vi. Research Responsibilities of Each Student

- To make group discussions effective, each student should be given a topic or subtopic to research.
- Each student should make notes or simple points to share with the group.
- When each student does their part, it makes the discussion go faster, and everyone learns a lot in the shortest possible time.

- Example: different theories of education. Five students each pick one subtopic, and they should make notes to share with the group.

vii. The Day of Discussion

- On the day of discussion, one student should remember to text all the members about the time and venue. Lateness should be avoided as much as possible. Everyone should be ready and prepared.
- If someone cannot make it due to an emergency, they should notify other members.

- If the group has a leader, they can send messages to everyone about what is expected of them that day.
- Members should be notified if any changes occur, like the library being closed early.

d. Learning by Points

- Learning by points means you have summarized all of your notes. In my book, I call this summary your *book of remembrance*. (Refer to chapter 2.)
- You take important points that are vital to the subject being considered. Write them in a small booklet, and carry it with you all the time.
- If you are studying genetics, summarize important points like the meaning of DNA, gene dominance, recessive genes, mutations, and so forth.
- Write the definition for all of them, or summarize Gregor Mendel's explanation into simple points.

DNA: deoxyribonucleic acid

Dominant Gene: a segment of DNA information used to make chromosomes

Recessive Gene: an allele that is only expressed in the phenotype of an organism if there are no dominant alleles present

Mutation: a change in the sequence of DNA bases which changes the genetic code

Phenotype: the physical expression of genes which results from both the environment and the genotype of the organism

e. Read in Advance

- Reading in advance is the right thing to do. When I was in college, I went to my professors to be registered for their class and for materials, contents, and topics for the semester. I will start to read in advance to gain prior knowledge of what will be done in class.
- That makes the class and learning easier. You are always ahead of the class. There is no stress. Get materials for the next class or lab, and study it over the weekend.
- Reading in advance in class will make you a good participant and not a stranger or spectator.

f. Solve Questions while You Study

Solving questions while you study is a good way to help you understand what you are learning. It gives you good feedback as to whether you understand the concept.

g. Make Drafts of Assignments

- Assignments are a way of showing you understood what was taught in class. It is feedback for your professor and isn't meant to bring students down or give them busywork.
- Most students think teachers punish them by giving them a lot of assignments, but that is not so. Most education systems are full of assignments to help students work hard and expand their levels of knowledge to improve understanding of the subject matter.
- When students complete assignments on time, it makes them more disciplined and prepares them for future careers in which there will be more to be done.

3. Other Key Strategies

a. Collaborate with Other Students

- Study with your friend and share ideas together.
- Difficult questions can be solved by your friends.
- Divide your labor by sharing notes or course materials and letting each person master small parts. Then share and discuss with each other.

b. Build Social Networks, and Join Clubs and Organization

- Try to build a social network with other students—especially senior course mates.
- Don't be in a hurry to leave after your classes, and spend some time getting to know about your classmates' lives.
- They can help you with old materials or even tell you what kinds of questions to expect from your professor.
- Join associations or clubs, like Teachers Helping Teachers on Facebook, where teachers share our studies, post questions, and discuss ideas.

c. Make Good Use of Available Research on How Students Learn

- There are several studies educators have done that identify how students learn.
- Find time to read about these articles, and see where you fit in. For example, students learn more when they are engaged or learn through visuals.
- Identify if you are nocturnal or diurnal.
- Identify whether you are more comfortable learning in the night or day time.
- Include other books, encyclopedias, websites, and learning centers.

d. Study at your favorite places.

- Find an appropriate place for your studies. The campuses of colleges are usually big, and not every place can be good for studying.
- Identify a convenient place such as a study room, library, or computer room in order to study effectively

CHAPTER FIVE

Preparing for
and Excelling
at Exams

---

1. How to Prepare for Exams

- Taking exams can come with fear and uncertainty.
- Most students become nervous days or weeks before exams for several individual, social, and cultural reasons.
- There's a need to overcome these challenges or mitigate them to the barest minimum.
- On the whole, students should strategically position themselves for exams.
- Learning and adequately preparing ahead of time and avoiding piling up lots of material only to study at the last minute will not help.
- This circumstance will make you stressed.

2. On the Day of the Exams

- Make sure you get to the venue on time.

- Don't overlearn and stress yourself. Take it easy.
- You can scan through your remembrance booklet.
- Go through the objective of the course or what your professor wanted you to understand.
- Get a good breakfast.
- Get a good night's sleep.
- Relax, and don't be stressed out.
- Use the remembrance books and drawings.
- Avoid unnecessary conversations with friends and family.
- Avoid quarreling, fighting, and arguments that lead to tension.
- Avoid things that can make you stressed, like checking your bank account for your paycheck that might not have arrived yet.
- Avoid watching television and spending lot of time on social media.

3. In the Week before the Exams

- Go through all the content and topics from lectures.
- Review quizzes and reports to learn from your mistakes.
- Attend any review sessions organized by your professor.
- Solve as many questions as possible, especially the professor's previous questions if there are any. The purpose of an exam is to make sure you've mastered the concept.
- Study the course outline to get an idea of what will be on the exam.
- Meet with your group discussion team to study together and review key points.

4. Months before the Exams

- Go through each topic in detail.
- Ask questions about anything you don't understand.
- Write and summarize your notes, and make them simpler.
- Do more of group discussion to gain understanding of the course material.

- Learn by writing to make sure you can remember easily.
- Draw diagrams or sketches with relevant information about the exams on the wall of your room or on your phone.

5. How to Answer Questions

- Raise your hand if you need help or need any clarification regarding a question.
- Use all available space on the answer sheet.
- Don't answer your question on the question sheet before you transfer onto the answer sheet. It's time consuming, which may prevent you from proofreading.
- Attend all review sessions with your professors so you can learn how to answer their questions.
- Read carefully, and know what the questions are about and what is expected of you.
- Analyze the questions, and try to understand before you answer.
- Follow the rules and steps involved in how to ensure it.
- Write in simple, clear sentences.
- Some questions can be tricky. Be careful to unravel the mystery behind each before you answer. Some questions are not straightforward.
- Give examples to explain your points where necessary.
- Read through your answers and correct all spelling mistakes and grammatical errors.
- Compare the questions to your answers, and be sure they correspond.
- Manage your time wisely—especially when dealing with multiple-choice questions.
- Always look at the clock and the number of questions left to see if you need to speed up.

6. Adhering to Instructions

- Do not take any prohibited materials with you to the exams.
- Don't speak to anyone during exams. If you have any questions, only speak to the examiner.
- Abstain from suspicious behavior before and during the examination.
- Wait for the examiner to commence the exams before you proceed.
- Do not write anything—not even your name—unless you are told to.
- Stop writing when the examiner asks you to.

7. During the Exams

- Write your name or enter any code given to you when told to do so before you start.
- Read through the guidelines or instructions, and know what is expected of you.
- Pay attention to all your supervisors and listen for any public announcements.
- Organize your thoughts, and write them down.
- Avoid unnecessary tension, stress, and anxiety.
- Use your time wisely.
- Skip difficult questions and attend to them later.
- Avoid unnecessary trips to the restroom that consume time.

8. Take Note of These During Exams

a. Write Your Name

- Write your full name clearly on the answer and question sheet before you start your exams.
- Shade available spaces that correspond to your name on the answer sheet.

b. Follow Instructions

- Each exam has instructions you should follow to successfully complete it.
- An example could be: Answer questions 1–40 on the answer sheet and the rest on the rest the space provided on the question paper.
- Another example could be: Do not start the exam until you are told to.

c. Do Not Cheat

- Do not do the unthinkable by copying or asking a classmate for an answer to a question
- The consequence might be expelling you from that class or removal from your college.
- That exam is not the end of the world, so do your best to write the answers you know and submit your paper.
- What you want to copy might be the wrong answer.

d. Write Clearly

- In the absence of computerized testing someone will have to read your handwriting.
- Professors want to see clear handwriting for easier grading.
- Be fast during exams, but write clearly to make sure the instructor will be able to read without any difficulty.
- Do your best to avoid unnecessary spelling mistakes that muddy the meanings of your sentences.
- Avoid long sentences that are difficult to understand.
- Use all punctuation correctly.

e. Answer All Compulsory Questions

- Some exam questions are designed to test students in a particular concept.
- Such questions are always compulsory on the test, so answer those questions first if possible.
- Compulsory questions may carry a lot of points, so make sure your answers are correct and well-written.

f. Go through Your Answers

- It is expedient for you to go through your answers before you submit your paper.
- Make sure all answers correspond to the question numbers.
- Make sure you shaded correctly on the answer sheet. Sometimes you see the answer as (a) and end up shading (b).
- Make sure you have answered all questions to the best of your knowledge, and correct all spelling mistakes.

g. Make Sure to Submit All Answer Sheets

- Stop working when it is time, and submit your answer sheet before you leave the exam room.
- Make sure you print your name as proof you wrote the exam.
- Some exams might require you to submit your questionnaire, and you'd do well to comply. They can disqualify you if you don't.

I wish all students the best in life and a very bright future.

I congratulate all students who are graduating.

Congratulations!

ACKNOWLEDGEMENTS

This book has come this far due to the assistance of people and agencies who have contributed by giving their time, talents, and ideas.

First I want to acknowledge the Mott Hall Science and Technology Academy in the Bronx, New York. Thank you to the founding principal, Dr. Patrick Awosogba—a great leader and a man of vision; assistant principal, Ms. Marcia Thomas; assistant principal, Ms. Mariam Ruiz; and dean, Ms. Jaymie Hernandez. Thank you also to my co-science and bilingual teacher, Mr. James Connors.

I thank the professors of the chemistry department at Bronx Community College for their academic support while I completed my major in Earth system and environmental sciences.

I am thankful to Professor Twum-Ampofo, my academic advisor and project supervisor of the Kwame Nkrumah University of Science and Technology and the faculty of renewable natural resource management in Kumasi-Ghana.

I am thankful to all professors and faculty of the University of California, Riverside, for their support while I was doing my global business certification program there—especially president Karen Diamond

Finally, thank you to the faculty and professors of the School of Education of City College of New York for helping me with my MA in secondary science education and certification.

SPECIAL THANKS

Special thanks to God for His help and wisdom while I wrote this book.

Special thanks to educational consultant Barbara Shut for her support and guidance. Barbara has been supporting me since my first book and has introduced me to all kinds of destiny helpers. Barbara you are the best.

I thank Dr. Leo Juma, professor of agriculture at Great Lakes University of Kisumu, Kenya, for forwarding my first book *Yes, I Can: Guidelines for Studies for High School Students.*

Thanks to professor Gregory Borman, a great lecturer at the secondary science education program at City College, and professor Richard Steinberg, head of secondary science education and all professors and faculty of City College of New York School of Education.

Thanks to professor Eugene Adams of collaborative educational programs of Bronx Community College, who forwarded my second book, and professor Neal Philip, chairman of the chemistry department of Bronx Community College.

I thank my head pastor and spiritual mother, prophetess Elizabeth Okrah Obeng, and her husband, overseer Jonathan Obeng. Together, they founded the Jehovah Rapha Prayer Ministry International for spiritual support. My gratitude goes to my spiritual father, apostle Sydney Quaye of Shekinah Avenue Ministry in Ghana, and also to Reverend Felicia Sarpong Gambrah and pastor Chika Nnadiri for their spiritual support and mentorship.

Thanks to Keegan Addo for taking the pictures in this book and to Kofi Sarfo for helping me type the manuscript.

Thank you to our college students and alumni who volunteered to use their personal planned schedules as examples for this book.

Finally, thank you to my brothers Evans Nyarko Kyere, Dr. Vincent Nartey Kyere, and Emmanuel Asenso Kyere.

Printed in the United States
by Baker & Taylor Publisher Services